Frida & Diego's Kitty Cookbook. Copyright © 2019. By Alessanda Luciano. All Rights Reserved. No part of this book may be reproduced in any manner without the express written consent of the author or publisher.

THIRTY-THREE & 1/3 PUBLISHING. Printed in the USA.

FAIR USE FOR EDUCATION AND RESEARCH. This book represents a culmination of materials, as related to preparation, storage and recommended uses of natural, organic and Non GMO Products as related to feline nutrition, whereas those works are utilized as a matter of public domain and further the Fair Use Act as it applies to education and research.

DISCLAIMER. The author does not in any way provide a guarantee or a warranty, express or implied, towards the content of recipes in this book. It is the reader's responsibility to determine the value and quality of any recipe or instructions provided for food preparation and to determine the nutritional value for your pet, if any, and safety of the preparation instructions. The recipes presented are intended for educational, informational and entertainment purposes and for use by persons having appropriate technical skill, at their own discretion and risk.

Further, the author is not liable, not responsible and does not assume obligation for:
- Adverse reactions to food consumed such as food poisoning and any kind of food-borne disease
- Misinterpreted recipe
- Domestic accidents, including but not limited to fires in your kitchen or cuts for example.
- Any food related allergic reactions your pet could have when trying a new food.
- Any pet related accidents that could occur when introducing a new food item to your pet.

The author does not make any warranties for the outcome of your food experiments. Before trying a new recipe, make sure your pet is not allergic to any of the ingredients. Use the right amounts and tools. What you decide to do with the recipes here is your responsibility.

ISBN-13: 978-194-8909-433

Frida & Diego's Kitty Cookbook

Assembled by their human

Alessandra Luciano

Recipes & Advise for Making

Certified Organic

All-Natural ~ Non-GMO

Cat Cookies, Biscuits & Treats

I dedicate this culmination

of recipes to you

Frida and Diego

Contents

Introduction ~ 9

GMO Facts ~ 15

Natural, Human Grade & Organic ~ 31

Frida & Diego's Recipes ~ 39

    Crunchy Beef Cubes ~ 45
    Chewy Liver Strips ~ 47
    Liver Biscuits ~ 49
    Turkey Bites ~ 51
    Turkey Wedges ~ 53
    Canned Cat Food Treats ~ 55
    Cat Attack Cookies ~ 57
    Kitty Cat Crackers ~ 59
    Holiday Kitty Cookies ~ 61
    Kitty Yum Yums ~ 63
    Frida's Biscuits ~ 65
    Oyster Bites ~ 67
    Chicken Liver Balls ~ 69

Diego's Tuna Cookies ~ 71
Crunchy Mini Tuna Biscuits ~ 73
Salmon Kitty Treats ~ 75
Chewy Kitty Treats ~ 77
Chicken & Berry Catsicle ~ 79
Tuna Catsicle ~ 81
No Bake Kitty Kisses ~ 83
Spinach & Chicken Cat Biscuits ~ 85
Tuna Cookies ~ 87

Frida & Diego's Superfoods ~ 89

Dangerous Foods ~ 97

Grain Free ~ 109

Pottenger's Cats ~ 115

Resources ~ 129

Introduction

We all love our pets and want to ensure they have a long, healthy and happy life with us. Research shows that the number of pet health problems directly related to poor nutrition is increasing.

Luckily, there are a number of certified organic, non-GMO pet foods available.

When searching for an appropriate treats for Frida and Diego I became appalled at the lack of options and the ingredient lists on the treats being sold for pet consumption!

Pets love treats and pet parents love being able to offer them to their four-legged family members.

Unfortunately, the majority of commercial pet treats, while palatable for cats, are neither species-appropriate nor do they contain high quality ingredients.

In fact, most cat treats don't remotely resemble the cute and colorful cat treats you may be used to seeing on store shelves.

Forming treats into tiny cat or fish shapes, is nearly impossible and requires the use of undesirable ingredients like grains and other starches, not to mention fillers, preservatives, sugar, and other additives, to make that happen. I don't want those types of ingredients in Frida and Diego's foods. So my concern is not cookie shape fishes for her snacks.

As Frida and Diego's human mom, I am naturally concerned for her and I select the ingredients I use for these recipes very carefully. I am not only concerned that her diet is certified organic and non-GMO, I am concerned about the over all nutritional value of what she consumes on a daily basis. I realize that as a cat she has specific needs in order to have a long healthy and sustained life with me.

I also believe that Frida and Diego are cats. So their diet must be very different than mine and their portions must make sense relative to their tiny being. Obesity can impact their health and well, we don't want that. So remember these treats are not meals.

The bottom line is that Cats are "obligate carnivores". Obligate means "by necessity." So combining obligate with carnivore it becomes pretty clear. Cats must eat meat;

it is a biological necessity for them.

I am not vet. And I am not even a nutritionist. I am Frida and Diego's human mom. So I have no gain in this process other than wanting them both to have a balanced healthy diet just like most humans want for their own children. It is just something a cat parent worries about.

There are serveral sections of this book unreated to recipes. That is because I feel it is important to become informed about the food supply and specific ingredient options we have for ourselves and our pets. If you don't want to read those sections that is okay too. Every pet owner should do their own due diligence and research what works best for their pet and family member.

The information I have gathered and am sharing with you is what works best for Firda and Diego, coupled with my own personal beliefs. That does not mean it will all be right for you and your pet. Pick and choose what you like.

Be sure to discuss your options and concerns with your pet's veterinarian and do your own research, using this book as a starting point for a broader discussion and an awakening in the world of responsible pet care.

Take a look at the section at the back on SUPERFOODS (Page 89) for your pet and consider ways to incorporate those into your pets diet.

The pictures used on the front and back cover of this book are actually of Frida and Diego.

I hope these recipes, tips and ideas will inspire you to make those treat calories count by offering nutritious, biologically appropriate snacks to your feline family member.

Good Luck with the recipes and happy treat making!

GMO Facts

What are GMOs?

GMOs (or "genetically modified organisms") are living organisms whose genetic material has been artificially manipulated in a laboratory through genetic engineering, or GE. This relatively new science creates unstable combinations of plant, animal, bacteria and viral genes that do not occur in nature or through traditional crossbreeding methods.

Virtually all commercial GMOs are engineered to withstand direct application of herbicide and/or to produce an insecticide. Despite biotech industry promises, none of the GMO traits currently on the market offer increased yield, drought tolerance, enhanced nutrition, or any other consumer benefit.

Meanwhile, there is a growing body of evidence connecting GMOs with health problems, environmental damage and violation of farmers' and consumers' rights.

Are GMOs safe?

Most developed nations do not consider GMOs to be safe for human consumption. So why would be want to feed GMOs to our pets? In more than 60 countries around the world, including Australia,

Japan and all of the countries in the European Union, there are significant restrictions or outright bans on the production and sale of GMOs. In the U.S., the government has approved GMOs based on studies conducted by the same corporations that created them and profit from their sale. Increasingly, Americans are taking matters into their own hands and choosing to opt out of the GMO experiment.

"Any politician or scientist who tells you these products are safe is either very stupid or lying. The hazards of these foods are uncertain. In view of our enormous ignorance, the premature application of biotechnology is downright dangerous. - David Suzuki, CC, OBC, Ph.D LLD, Geneticist."

<u>What about our pets?</u>

We all love our pets and want to ensure they have a long, healthy life with us. Research shows that the number of pet health problems directly related to poor nutrition is increasing. Luckily, there are a number of certified organic, non-GMO pet foods available. Talk to your veterinarian for detailed information on providing a balanced diet for your pet.

Become informed

The Non-GMO Project is a non-profit organization committed to preserving and building the non-GMO food supply, educating consumers, and providing verified non-GMO choices. Everyone deserves an informed choice about whether or not to consume genetically modified organisms. The Non-GMO Project has a beautiful website and provide much needed information to protect our health and that of our feline family members. The web site is: nongmoproject.org

More about the Non-GMO Project

The Non-GMO Project was created by leaders representing all sectors of the organic and natural products industry in the U.S. and Canada, to offer consumers a consistent non-GMO choice for organic and natural products that are produced without genetic engineering or recombinant DNA technologies.

The US does not currently require labeling of food products made with genetically modified ingredients (GMOs).

How can you make an informed choice if GM ingredients aren't clearly listed on the label?

Look for the Non-GMO Project verified seal. The guiding mission of the Non-GMO Project is the belief that consumers in North America should have access to clearly labeled non-GMO food and products in the marketplace.

The Non-GMO Project offers North America's only independent verification for products made according to best practices for GMO avoidance.

The Project was conceived by retailers, who wanted an easy, consistent way to help shoppers see which products were committed to non-GMO ingredients.

Prior to the Project, there was no consistency in non-GMO labeling claims. Manufacturers made claims according to their own internal criteria, which ranged from rigorous to meaningless, either way offered no transparency to the consumer.

Unlike many "absence claims" made about GMO content (e.g. "GMO free"), the Non-GMO Project offers a truthfully worded claim, "Non-GMO Project Verified."

This claim and seal offers a true statement acknowledging the reality of contamination risk - stating simply that the product in question has been "verified" by the Project.

A brand's enrollment in the Project gives them a way to share their diligence in producing food according to consensus-based best practices for GMO avoidance, including testing of risk ingredients with you in a valid, meaningful way.

Are you still feeding your pets GMOs?

Many pet owners have connected the rise of GMOs with what seems to be an increased amount of tumors in pets, including dogs and cats.

There has been a lack of studies as to the numbers surrounding tumors in pets, so the causes remain unknown, but it is well worth noting that many farmers have reported similar ailments in their animals fed GMOs, and studies have shown the same in lab animals.

It's pretty commonplace to see lower quality ingredients in pet food than human food, but that doesn't mean you have to compromise and feed your pet dangerous, untested GMOs that could be greatly harming their health.

Non-GMO Pet Food Brands to Try

Most pet food, especially the big name brands, and even many "healthy" brands, contains GMOs, but the following brands are non-GMO Project Verified:

- Ascenta– It's no secret that cats do well on fish, and this company produces non-GMO verified Omega 3 fish oil supplements specifically for our feline friends.
- The Furry Foodie- Non-GMO Project Verified and mostly organic, the company's beef dinner for dogs is spotlighted on the project's website.
- Brad's Raw 4 Paws- This company has been quiet on Facebook and its website but is still listed on the Non-GMO Project Verified site as a possible option.
- Wild Wings– Offering Organic Non-GMO Verified Bird Foods, this company is worth a look for both pet owners and bird watchers/feeders alike.
- 4Legz– Made without the use of corn or wheat, these GMO-free treats are well worth a look.
- BioStar– With a line of foods for both dogs and horses, this company has a

unique selection of treats, supplements and many more items to optimize your pet's health. Includes blends for joint health, digestive health and much more.
- Nummy Tum Tum– Using wholesome ingredients like sweet potatoes and pumpkin, this non-GMO verified line boasts that it's ideal for all pets (it even says so on the can).
- DooKashi– This brand is not food, but it's non-GMO probiotic blend can help pet owners by eliminating cat litter box odors.

For more information see the full Non-GMO Project Verified Website at nongmoprojcet.org and *please be aware that these products may still contain trace amounts of contamination.*

When shopping look for this Label:

List of genetically modified foods

It's virtually impossible to provide a complete list of genetically modified food (GM food) in the United States because there aren't any laws for governing genetically modified crops!

Some estimates say as many *as 30,000 d*ifferent products on grocery store shelves are "modified." That's largely because many processed foods contain soy. Half of North America's soy crop is genetically engineered!

Rapeseed - Resistance to certain pesticides and improved rapeseed cultivars to be free of erucic acid and glucosinolates. Gluconsinolates, which were found in rapeseed meal leftover from pressing, are toxic and had prevented the use of the meal in animal feed. In Canada, where "double-zero" rapeseed was developed, the crop was renamed "canola" (Canadian oil) to differentiate it from non-edible rapeseed.

Honey - Honey can be produced from GM crops. Some Canadian honey comes from bees collecting nectar from GM canola plants. This has shut down exports of Canadian honey to Europe.

Cotton - Resistant to certain pesticides - considered a food because the oil can be consumed. The introduction of genetically engineered cotton plants has had an unexpectedly effect on Chinese agriculture. The so-called Bt cotton plants that produce a chemical that kills the cotton bollworm have not only reduced the incidence of the pest in cotton fields, but also in neighboring fields of corn, soybeans, and other crops.

Rice - Genetically modified to contain high amounts of Vitamin A. Rice containing human genes is to be grown in the US. Rather than end up on dinner plates, the rice will make human proteins useful for treating infant diarrhea in the developing world.

Soybean - Genetically modified to be resistant to herbicides - Soy foods including, soy beverages, tofu, soy oil, soy flour, lecithin. Other products may include breads, pastries, snack foods, baked products, fried products, edible oil products and special purpose foods.

Sugar Cane - Made resistant to certain pesticides. A large percentage of sweeteners used in processed food actually comes from corn, not sugar cane or beets. Genetically modified sugar cane is regarded so badly by consumers at the present time that it could not be marketed successfully.

Tomatoes - Made for a longer shelf life and to prevent a substance that causes tomatoes to rot and degrade.

Corn - Resistant to certain pesticides - Corn oil, flour, sugar or syrup. May include snack foods, baked goods, fried foods, edible oil products, confectionery, special purpose foods, and soft drinks.

Sweet Corn - genetically modified to produces its own insecticide. Officials from the US Food and Drug Administration (FDA) have said that thousands of tons of genetically engineered sweet corn have made their way into the human food supply chain, even though the produce has been approved only for use in animal feed. Recently Monsanto, a biotechnology food producer, said that about half of the USA's sweet corn acreage has been planted with genetically modified seed this year.

Canola - Canola oil. May include edible oil products, fried foods, baked products, and snack foods.

Potatoes - (Atlantic, Russett Burbank, Russet Norkatah, and Shepody) - May include snack foods, processed potato products and other processed foods containing potatoes.

Flax - More and more food products contain flax oil and seed because of their excellent nutritional properties. No genetically modified flax is currently grown. An herbicide-resistant GM flax was introduced in 2001, but was soon taken off the market because European importers refused to buy it.

Papaya - The first virus resistant papayas were commercially grown in Hawaii in 1999. Transgenic papayas now cover about one thousand hectares, or three quarters of the total Hawaiian papaya crop. Monsanto, donated technology to Tamil Nadu Agricultural University, Coimbatore, for developing a papaya resistant to the ring-spot virus in India.

Squash - (yellow crookneck) - Some zucchini and yellow crookneck squash are also GM but they are not popular with farmers.

Red-Hearted Chicory - (Radicchio) - Chicory (Cichorium intybus var. foliosum) is popular in some regions as a salad green, especially in France and Belgium. Scientists developed a genetically modified line of chicory containing a gene that makes it male sterile, simply facilitating the production of hybrid cultivars. Today there is no genetically modified chicory on the market.

Cotton Seed Oil - Cottonseed oil and linters. Products may include blended vegetable oils, fried foods, baked foods, snack foods, edible oil products, and small-goods casings.

Tobacco - The company Vector has a GMO tobacco being sold under the brand of Quest cigarettes in the U.S. It is engineered to produce low or no nicotine.

Meat - Meat and dairy products usually come from animals that have eaten GM feed.

Peas - Genetically modified (GM) peas created immune responses in mice, suggesting that they may also create serious allergic reactions in people. The peas had been inserted with a gene from kidney beans, which creates a protein that acts as a pesticide.

Vegetable Oil - Most generic vegetable oils and margarines used in restaurants and in processed foods in North America are made from soy, corn, canola, or cottonseed. Unless these oils specifically say "Non-GMO" or "Organic," it is probably genetically modified.

Sugar beets – Maybe included any processed foods containing sugar.

Dairy Products - About 22 percent of cows in the U.S. are injected with recombinant (genetically modified) bovine growth hormone (rbGH).

Vitamins - Vitamin C (ascorbic acid) is often made from corn, vitamin E is usually made from soy. Vitamins A, B2, B6, and B12 may be derived from GMOs as well as vitamin D and vitamin K may have "carriers" derived from GM corn sources, such as starch, glucose, and maltodextrin.

GM Crops List (Partial)

Alfalfa (Medicago sativa)
Apple (Malus x Domestica)
Argentine Canola (Brassica napus)
Bean (Phaseolus vulgaris)
Carnation (Dianthus caryophyllus)
Chicory (Cichorium intybus)
Cotton (Gossypium hirsutum L.)
Creeping Bentgrass (Agrostis stolonifera)
Eggplant (Solanum melongena)
Eucalyptus (Eucalyptus sp.)
Flax (Linum usitatissumum L.)
Maize (Zea mays L.)
Melon (Cucumis melo)
Papaya (Carica papaya)
Petunia (Petunia hybrida)
Plum (Prunus domestica)
Polish canola (Brassica rapa)
Poplar (Populus sp.)
Potato (Solanum tuberosum L.)
Rice (Oryza sativa L.)
Rose (Rosa hybrida)
Soybean (Glycine max L.)
Squash (Cucurbita pepo)
Sugar Beet (Beta vulgaris)
Sugarcane (Saccharum sp)
Sweet pepper (Capsicum annuum)
Tobacco (Nicotiana tabacum L.)
Tomato (Lycopersicon esculentum)
Wheat (Triticum aestivum)

Natural, Human Grade & Certified Organic

What does Natural, Human Grade and Organic mean - really?

Pet Stores are selling more and more cat foods labeled "natural," "human grade" and "organic," and the industry considers them to be the hot new trend.

Because the government has never defined "natural" for human foods, this word essentially means anything the manufacturer says it does. For pet foods, however, the Association of American Feed Control Officials (AAFCO) has an official definition:

Natural:

"A feed or ingredient derived solely from plant, animal or mined sources, either in it's unprocessed state or having been subject to physical processing, heat processing, rendering, purification, extraction, hydrolysis, enzymolysis or fermentation, but not having been produced by or subject to a chemically synthetic process and not containing any additives or processing aids that are chemically synthetic except in amounts as may occur unavoidably in good manufacturing processes."

AAFCO also says that "natural" must not mislead; if it appears on the label, every ingredient in the product must meet the definition. But even AAFCO knows this is impossible. Pet food companies typically buy vitamins, minerals and other additives from factories overseas, where, as we learned in last year's pet food recalls, quality controls are sometimes nonexistent.

There are not a lot of companies claiming to use human-grade ingredients on their package labels, mainly because AAFCO does not have an official definition of the term. Without an approved AAFCO definition, an ingredient or term is not supposed to be used on pet food labels.

AAFCO says "human-grade" is false and misleading, and constitutes misbranding, unless every ingredient in the product—and every processing method—meets FDA and USDA requirements for producing, processing and transporting foods suitable for consumption by humans, and every producer of the ingredients is licensed to perform those tasks. Few pet food companies can meet these criteria.

Only a few other companies make human-grade claims on their food labels, but many use the term freely in their in-store materials and website advertising.

For example, Newman's Own Organics presents this information in a question-and-answer format: "Q: Does Newman's Own Organics use human grade materials? Why isn't that written on the bag? A: Newman's Own Organics organic pet food uses human grade and fit for human consumption ingredients such as natural chicken and organic grains. The AAFCO Board ... actually prohibits the printing of 'Human Grade' on pet food packaging."

That brings us to organics.

For human foods, "organic" has a precise meaning defined by the USDA's National Organic Program (NOP).

"To be certified as organic, plant ingredients in pet foods must be grown without pesticides, artificial fertilizers, genetic modification, irradiation or sewage sludge. Animal ingredients must come from animals raised on organic feed, given access to the outdoors, and not treated with antibiotics or hormones. Producers must be inspected to make sure they adhere to these standards."

AAFCO says that:

(1) under NOP rules, pet foods may not display the USDA organic seal or claim that they were produced according to organic standards.

but (2), NOP also says labeling terms such as "100% organic," "organic" or "made with organic ingredients" on pet foods may be truthful and do not imply organic production or certification.

And therefore (3), AAFCO recommends that labeling rules for human foods apply to pet foods.

Bottom line, you can go into any pet food store and easily find products that violate these standards.

A marketing twist to look out for when shopping for commercial pet food, is that there are companies out there that just call themselves organic when their foods do not contain a single organic ingredient. They get away with this because the USDA, unlike the FDA, doesn't regulate company names.

At the moment, "organic" means something for human food; it does not mean much for pet food. We worry that the USDA doesn't think pet foods are important enough to care what is said on their labels.

Research, research and research.

Frida & Diego's Recipes

Recipe Index

Crunchy Beef Cubes ~ 45
Chewy Liver Strips ~ 47
Liver Biscuits ~ 49
Turkey Bites ~ 51
Turkey Wedges ~ 53
Canned Cat Food Treats ~ 55
Cat Attack Cookies ~ 57
Kitty Cat Crackers ~ 59
Holiday Kitty Cookies ~ 61
Kitty Yum Yums ~ 63
Frida's Biscuits ~ 65
Oyster Bites ~ 67
Chicken Liver Balls ~ 69
Diego's Tuna Cookies ~ 71
Crunchy Mini Tuna Biscuits ~ 73
Salmon Kitty Treats ~ 75
Chewy Kitty Treats ~ 77
Chicken & Berry Catsicle ~ 79
Tuna Catsicle ~ 81
No Bake Kitty Kisses ~ 83
Spinach & Chicken Cat Biscuits ~ 85
Tuna Cookies ~ 87

SPECIAL CONSIDERATION:

ALL RECIPES call for the use of Non-GMO, Certified, all natural, Organic ingredients.

Going to the grocery can be overwhelming. To make shopping easier look for the following key terms when shopping:

- NON GMO Verified Products
- Organic Grass Fed Beef
- Organic Free Range Eggs
- Organic No Salt Added Butter without Artificial Growth Hormones (rBST)
- First cold-pressed Organic Extra Virgin Olive Oil
- Non GMO Salmon
- Kabrita Non GMO Verified Goat Milk
- Organic Non GMO Goat Cheese
- Organic Non GMO Fruit or Veggies

Crunchy Beef Cubes

Ingredients

- 1 pound lean Organic Grass Fed Beef
- Baking sheet covered with baking parchment

Instructions:

- Dice beef into half-inch cubes
- Place cubes close together on baking sheet
- Put baking sheet into cold oven and heat oven to 300° F
- Cook for 1 hour
- Reduce oven temperature to 200° F and prop open oven door (to allow moisture to escape) and continue cooking for 2 additional hours
- Remove beef cubes from oven and allow to dry overnight at room temperature.

- Place beef cubes in airtight container and keep refrigerated or frozen until ready to serve.

Chewy Liver Strips

Ingredients

- Organic Grass Fed Beef Livers - Butcher shops sometimes throw these away or you can buy them at the supermarket. Better yet find a local organic farmer!
- Food dehydrator*

Instructions

- Cut liver into 1-inch slices
- Apply a non-stick spray on the dehydrator drying racks
- Place the liver slices into the dehydrator for 24 hours
- Seal in airtight container and refrigerate or freeze until ready to serve
- An alternative to using a food dehydrator is to put the liver strips on a greased or non-stick baking sheet and bake them in a 325° F oven for 45 minutes to an hour.

Liver Biscuits

Ingredients

- 1 pound Organic Grass Fed Beef Liver
- 1 large Organic Free Range Egg
- 1 ¼ cups Organic Potato Flakes
- Organic Beef or Chicken Broth
- Food Processor
- Greased 13 x 9 pan

Instructions

- Preheat oven to 400° F
- Cut liver into approximately 1-inch pieces (to help with the blending and cooking process)
- Place the liver pieces, egg, and potato flakes in food processor
- Pulse ingredients to combine
- Add as much broth as needed to make the mixture spreadable (the consistency will be very thick)
- Spread mixture into pan
- Bake for 25 minutes; cool on wire rack for 5 minutes

- Loosen sides with a knife, turn pan over and empty mixture onto wire rack
- Cool completely before slicing
- Place slices in airtight container and refrigerate or freeze until ready to serve.

Turkey Bites

Ingredients

- 1 pound Ground Free Range Organic Turkey
- 1 large Organic Free Range Egg
- 1 teaspoon chopped Fresh Parsley
- ¼ cup Shredded Organic Goat Cheese (optional)
- ½ cup Chopped Organic Non-GMO Veggies (optional)

Instructions

- Preheat oven to 350° F
- Mix all ingredients in bowl
- Shape mixture into bite-size balls
- Bake for 10 minutes or until brown
- Cool and serve or seal in airtight container and store in fridge or freezer until ready to serve.

Turkey Wedges

Ingredients

- 1 large Organic Free Range Brown Egg
- 1 to 2 tablespoons mashed potatoes
- ½ cup diced cooked Free Range Organic Turkey Meat
- ½ cup Chopped Cooked Organic Non-GMO Veggies
- ¼ cup Grated Organic Goat Cheese

Instructions

- Warm a small amount of olive oil in a medium-sized skillet.
- Blend the egg and potatoes in a bowl and then spread in the skillet.
- Lay the turkey and veggies on top in even layers. Cover and simmer until the egg is cooked and the mixture is warm
- Sprinkle cheese on top of mixture and cook a few more minutes until cheese is melted and egg is golden brown.

- Cool, cut into wedges
- Put in fridge or freezer until ready to serve.

Frozen Treats from Canned Pet Food

If you buy commercial canned food for cat, you can turn it into a supply of healthy kitty treats. (Depending on the brand of cat food you purchase in a can).

Ingredients

- One can of your cats Organic Non-GMO pet food
- Parchment paper

Instructions

- Open a can of your pet's favorite brand, preferably something with a strong aroma, and spoon out little treat sized amounts onto a baking sheet covered with parchment paper.
- Put the baking sheet into the freezer until the bite sized bits of food are frozen.
- Then move them to an airtight container and back into the freezer

they go until you're ready to treat your pet to a treat!
- You will need to thaw them to a chewy consistency for kitties.

Cat Attack Cookies

Ingredients

- 1 Cup Organic Non-GMO Whole wheat flour
- 1/4 Cup of Organic Non-GMO Soy flour
- 1 teaspoon of Organic Catnip
- 1 Organic Free Range Brown Egg
- 1/3 Cup Organic Goats Milk or Cat's Milk
- 2 Tablespoons Organic Non-GMO Wheat Germ
- 1/3 Cup Powdered Organic Goats Milk
- 1 Tablespoon Natural Non-GMO Unsulfured Molasses
- 2 Tablespoons Organic No Salt Added Butter without Artificial Growth Hormones (rBST)

Instructions

- Preheat oven to 350° F.
- Mix dry ingredients together. Add molasses, egg, butter and milk.

- Roll out flat onto oiled cookie sheet and cut into small, cat bite-sized pieces.
- Bake for 20 minutes.
- Let cool and store in tightly sealed container.

Kitty Cat Crackers

Ingredients

- 6 Ounces Undrained Non-GMO Canned Tuna
- 1 Cup Organic Non-GMO Cornmeal
- 1 Cup Organic Non-GMO Flour
- 1/3 Cup Water

Instructions

- Preheat the oven to 350° F.
- Measure all of the ingredients into a bowl and mix thoroughly with your hands.
- Roll out to 1/4 inch thickness and cut into treat sized pieces.
- Place on a greased cookie sheet and bake for about 20 minutes or until golden.
- Let cool.

Holiday Kitty Cookies

Ingredients

- 1 Can Non GMO Salmon or minced Organic Free Range Turkey meat
- 1/2 Cup Mashed cooked Organic Non-GMO Pumpkin
- 1 teaspoon First cold-pressed Organic Extra Virgin Olive Oil
- 1 teaspoon Organic Non-GMO Kelp

Instructions

- Mix together and roll into balls.
- Store in refrigerator after making.
- Let reach room temperature before serving.
- Feed in treat sized portions not as a meal.

Kitty Yum Yums

Ingredients

1/2 Cup of Dry Organic Grain Free Cat Food
¼ Cup Warm Water
3 Tablespoons Organic Catnip

Instructions

- Preheat oven to 350° F.
- Put the cat food and water in the bowl and mix well. Drain any excess water.
- Sprinkle the catnip over the mixture and mix well.
- Bake in a 350° F oven for 15 minutes.

Frida Biscuits

Ingredients

- 1-1/2 cups Organic Non GMO Whole Wheat Flour
- 1-1/2 tsp. Organic catnip (or substitute your cat's favorite organic Non Gmo ingredient tuna or bonito flakes) for the catnip)
- 1/3 cup dry Organic Goat's milk
- 2 Tablespoons melted Organic No Salt Added Butter without Artificial Growth Hormones (rBST)
- 1 Tablespoon Raw, locally made, Certified Organic Honey
- 1 large Organic Free Range Brown Egg

Instructions

- Preheat the oven to 350 ° F.
- Combine dry ingredients in a mixing bowl.
- Add wet ingredients and mix to form dough.

- Roll out, adding more flour if needed, and cut into squares or small shapes.
- Bake for approximately 20 minutes.
- Remove from oven, cool completely.
- Store in an airtight container, or freeze and thaw as needed.

 Oyster Biscuits

Ingredients

- 1 (3.75-oz.) can Natural Organic Oysters
- 6 baby Organic Non-GMO Carrots
- 2 Tablespoon Organic Tomato Paste
- 1 large Organic Free Range Brown Egg
- 1/3 cup plain, unseasoned organic Non-Gmo Bread Crumbs
- 2 teaspoon Organic Brewer's Yeast

Instructions

- Preheat the oven to 350 ° F.
- Place the oysters, carrots and tomato paste in a food processor or blender; puree until they form a smooth paste.
- In a mixing bowl, combine the pureed mixture and the remaining ingredients, mixing well.
- Drop by 1/2 teaspoonful onto a greased cookie sheet.
- Bake for 8 to 12 minutes or until the bottoms of the treats are golden

brown.
- Flip the treats and bake for another five minutes or until both sides are golden brown.
- Remove from the oven, let cool thoroughly and store in an airtight container in the refrigerator.

Chicken Liver Balls

Ingredients

- 1 lb. finely chopped cooked Organic Free Range Chicken Livers
- 1 cup Organic Non-GMO Cornmeal
- 3/4 cup all-purpose Organic Non-GMO Flour
- 2 Large Free Range Organic Brown Eggs
- 1/4 cup Organic Chicken Broth

Instructions

- Preheat the oven to 350 ° F.
- Combine all the ingredients, making sure the chicken liver is well-coated. The dough should be stiff, but if it's too dry, add a little more chicken broth.
- Form the dough into pea- to marble-sized balls and place on a greased cookie sheet.
- With the tip of a spoon, press a tiny indentation into the top of each ball.
- With a spoon, carefully drip a few

drops of chicken broth in each indentation.
- Bake the treats for 8 to 10 minutes or until the bottoms of the treats are golden brown.
- Remove from the oven, let cool thoroughly and store in an airtight container in the refrigerator.

Diego's Tuna Cookies

Ingredients

- 1 cup Organic Non-Gmo Whole-wheat flour
- 1 6-ounce can Non-GMO Tuna in oil (do not drain)
- 1 tablespoon First Cold-pressed Organic Extra Virgin Olive Oil
- 1 Organic Free Range Brown Egg

Instructions

- Mix all ingredients in a mixing bowl,
- Adding a little water if dough is too stiff.
- On a lightly-floured surface, roll dough to 1/4 inch thickness.
- Cut into shapes with your favorite cookie cutter, or use a pizza cutter to cross-cut into small diamond shapes.
- Place on ungreased baking sheet.
- Bake at 350 ° F for 20 minutes or until firm. Store in an airtight container.

Crunchy Mini Tuna Biscuits

Ingredients

- 1 (5 ounce) can Non-GMO tuna, no salt added and packed in water, drained
- 1 cup Organic Non-GMO oat flour***
- 1 tablespoon First Cold-pressed Organic Extra Virgin Olive Oil
- 1 Organic Free Range Brown Egg
- 1 heaping tablespoon dried Organic Catnip

Instructions

- Place a rack in the upper third of the oven and preheat oven to 350 ° F. Line a baking sheet with parchment paper and set aside.
- In the bowl of a food processor fitted with a blade attachment, combine drained tuna, oat flour, egg, olive oil and catnip. Blend until mixture is

smooth. It will be thick but pliable and not terribly sticky.
- Roll dough into 1/2 teaspoon balls and place on prepared cookie sheet.
- Use a skewer to press an X-shape into each cookie ball.
- Bake cookies for 10 to 12 minutes until they are dried on top and slightly browned.
- Allow to cool completely before offering to your kitty.
- Place treats in an airtight container and store in the refrigerator for up to seven days.

***It's easy to make your own oat flour. Simply grind organic non-gmo old-fashioned oats in a spice grinder until it is transformed into a light powder.

Salmon Kitty Treats

Ingredients

- 10 oz. canned Wild caught Non-GMO salmon (undrained)
- 1 Free Range Organic Egg (beaten)
- 2 cups Organic Non-GMO Whole Wheat Flour

Instructions

- Pre-Heat oven to 350°.
- Pulse 10 oz. canned salmon (undrained) in a food processor and chop as finely as possible.
- In a stand mixer, combine salmon, 1 egg (beaten) and 2 cups whole wheat flour until dough forms.
- If dough is too dry, add up to 1/3 cup water. If dough is too wet or sticky, add a bit more flour. Dough should be tacky but not sticky.
- Roll out dough on a floured surface until about 1/4 inch thick. Use a 3/4-

inch cookie cutter in the shape of your choice to create your treats.
- Place treats on a parchment-lined baking sheet and bake at 350° for about 20 minutes. When they're slightly browned and crunchy, they're done.
- Allow to cool before serving.
- Store in an airtight container for up to 2 weeks.

Chewy Cat Treats

Ingredients

- 1 large Free Range Organic Brown Egg
- 1 4-oz jar organic chicken and brown rice baby food (or something meaty which may include canned wet human grade cat food)
- 1/4 cup Fresh Parsley, coarsely chopped
- 2 teaspoons First cold-pressed Organic Extra Virgin Olive Oil
- 2 tablespoons water
- 1 cup Organic Non-GMO Bown Rice Flour
- 1/2 cup cooked organic Non-GMO Brown Rice
- Other Ingredients: Consider adding catnip or a Superfood.

Instructions

- Place a rack in the middle of the oven and preheat oven to 325° F.
- Line a baking sheet with parchment

paper and set aside.
- In a medium bowl, whisk together egg, baby food (or wet cat food), parsley, olive oil, and water.
- Add brown rice flour and cooked rice. Stir to incorporate. The mixture will be thick but spreadable.
- Spread mixture onto prepared baking sheet creating a rectangle that is about 1/3 of an inch thick.
- Bake for 12 to 15 minutes.
- Remove from the oven. Let rest until cool enough to handle, then slice soft dough into bite-sized pieces.
- Return pieces to the oven to bake for another 8 minutes.
- Remove from the oven. Allow to cool completely.
- Store in an airtight container in the refrigerator.

Chicken & Berry Catsicles

"A catsicile is a popsicle but for your cat!"

Ingredients

- Ice Cube Trays or Small Dixie Cups
- 1 5.5-ounce can of your cat's Organic, Chicken Non-GMO or Human Grade favorite wet food (smooth, not chunky, works best)
- Organic Catnip and/or soft Superfoods like Blueberries
- One small square of Saran Wrap

Instructions

- Mix cat food and optional superfood ingredients in a medium-sized bowl.
- The mix should be primarily cat food, with treats mixed in about the same ratio as you would when you make human cookies.
- Fill each Dixie Cup or Ice Cube Tray opening with about 1/4-1/2 inch of the mixture.

- Flatten the mixture by stacking one Dixie cup inside another or mashing it down with a small spoon.
- Place Saran Wrap over the top cup to avoid freezer burn.
- Place it in the freezer over night.
- The Next morning, run the bottom of the Dixie cup under warm tap water until you can pull it free of the other cups and pop out the catsicle.
- Place the catsicle inside a deep bowl to avoid messes and let stand about five minutes until the outside starts to sweat before giving it to your kitty.

 **Tuna Catsicles**

Ingredients

- 1 Can of Non-GMO Tuna
- 32 ounces of plain or Vanilla Organic Non GMO Goat Yogurt
- A blender
- Dixie cups or Ice Cube Trays

Instructions

- Blend all ingredients, including the water from the can of tuna, in a blender or food processor until creamy and smooth.
- Pour the blended ingredients into Dixie cups or in Ice Cube Trays and freeze over night or until solid.
- When they are ready to serve, cut the paper of one of the Dixie cups and pop the Popsicle out onto a paper plate or deep bowl or pop them out of the ice cube trays.
- Only serve kitty one treat and store

the rest for a later date in a freezer zip lock baggie.

No Bake Kitty Kisses

Ingredients

- 1/4 cup Organic Non-GMO Oats
- 1/3 cup Organic Non-GMO Peas (canned or thawed/frozen)
- 1/2 cup can of Non GM) Tuna (not drained)
- 1 tablespoons Shredded Organic Goat Cheese
- 2 teaspoons First cold-pressed Organic Extra Virgin Olive Oil

Instructions

- Combine all ingredients into food processor.
- Add only enough olive oil as necessary to make a dough.
- Puree in food processor
- Shape into 1/2" diameter small balls and keep refrigerated.

Spinach and Chicken Kitty Cat Biscuits

Ingredients

- 1/2 lb. Organic Boneless Free Range Skinless Chicken thighs
- 1 cup Non-GMO Organic Fresh Spinach
- 1 Large Egg, Organic Brown Free Range
- 1 cup Organic Non-GMO Quick Cooking Oats,
- 1/4 cup Organic Non-GMO Flour
- 1 tablespoon Organic Catnip

Instructions

- Preheat your oven to 350° F. Steam the boneless and skinless chicken thighs until cooked through.
- Note: You can swap for boneless and skinless organic chicken breasts, with Non-GMO Salmon or Tuna depending on your cats preference.
- Let the chicken cool for 20 minutes

before the next step.
- Place the chicken, oats, spinach leaves, egg, and catnip in a blender or food processor, and pulse on low until the mixture blends together.
- It should still be a bit chunky but also smooth, similar to the texture of wet sand.
- Pop the mixture into a bowl and add the flour. You can also add a dash of salt or sugar to mix up the flavor. Use your hands to knead the dough until it's no longer sticky, then place on a flour-dusted work surface.
- Use a rolling pin to create a rectangle of dough around 1/2 inch thick. With the help of a pizza cutter or small cookie cutter, create small shapes for the finished treats.
- Place the kitty treats on a parchment-lined sheet tray, and bake for 20 minutes.
- Remove from the oven, cool until room temperature, and then toss to your cat.

Tuna Cookies

Ingredients

- 1 cup Organic Non-GMO Whole-wheat flour
- 1 6-ounce can Non-GMO Tuna in oil (do not drain)
- 1 tablespoon oil
- 1 Organic Free Range Brown Egg

Instructions

- Mix all ingredients in a mixing bowl, adding a little water if dough is too stiff.
- On a lightly-floured surface, roll dough to 1/4 inch thickness.
- Cut into shapes with your favorite cookie cutter, or use a pizza cutter to cross-cut into small diamond shapes.
- Place on ungreased baking sheet.
- Bake at 350° F for 20 minutes or until firm.
- Store in an airtight container.

Frida & Diego's Superfoods

Superfoods for your cat?

Why not I ask? Why not. "Superfoods" are foods that are nutritionally dense, have minimum calories, and may help prevent disease and promote overall health.

There are several human superfoods that you can easily share with your feline companion. You can add them to your pet's meal, or offer them as snacks or training treats. If possible, buy locally grown, non-GMO, certified organic food.

Remember to go slowly when introducing new foods. And we recommend checking with your veterinarian first if your cat has any digestive issues or other health concerns. You should always discuss any nutritional needs with your kitty's veterinarian so that you are comfortable before incorporating any of the following superfoods to your pets diet.

Superfoods can be added to the recipes in this book and are great treats. So what are superfoods? I believe that humans need superfoods and so of course so does Frida!

Frida's Favorite Ten

1. Blueberries are available all year, and whether fresh or frozen, are great training treats for your feline companion. They are loaded with phytochemicals, and their deep blue hue is the result of anthocyanidins, which are powerful antioxidants. Blueberries are also a good source of healthy fiber, manganese, and vitamins C and E.

Take care to slowly introduce this superfood to your cat, as too much too soon can cause digestive upset. Replacing one of the current treats you feed each day with fresh or frozen blueberries is a great way to increase antioxidants.

2. **Broccoli** supports detoxification processes in your cat's body (and yours); contains healthy fiber to aid digestion; is rich in beneficial nutrients like potassium, calcium, protein and vitamin C; has anti-inflammatory properties; supports eye health; helps repair skin damage; and supports heart health.

If you cannot get organic produce, conventionally grown broccoli is one of the cleanest (most pesticide-free) foods you can buy, so eat up! Your pet may prefer broccoli steamed, although many cats eat florets fresh, with no problems. Chopped broccoli stems make great detox treats, too.

3. Chia is a seed derived from the desert plant Salvia hispanica that grows abundantly in southern Mexico. It is a source of plant-based omega-3 fatty acids and also antioxidants. And unlike flax seeds, chia seeds don't need to be ground. Chia seeds also provide fiber, calcium, phosphorus, magnesium, manganese, copper, iron, molybdenum, niacin, and zinc.

Try sprinkling some chia seeds on your cats's meals, or mix some with a little coconut oil for a super nutrient dense bedtime snack.

4. **Fermented vegetables.** Some cats love them; others won't even touch them!

Fermented foods are potent detoxifiers and contain much higher levels of probiotics and vitamin K2 than supplements can provide. Beneficial gut bacteria provided by probiotics break down and eliminate heavy metals and other toxins from the body, and perform a number of other important functions. Adding 1-3 teaspoons of fermented veggies to your pet's food each day (depending on body weight) is a great way to offer food-based probiotics and natural nutrients.

5. **Goji berries** are typically sold dried and resemble red raisins. Whole goji berries can be found at Chinese herbal shops, health food stores and almost all groceries. The berries are rich in amino acids and antioxidants, particularly carotenoids such as beta-carotene and zeaxanthin. Goji extracts may prevent the growth of cancer cells, reduce blood glucose, and lower cholesterol levels. I use these as tiny training rewards in place of processed cat treats with great success.

6. **Kale** is a dark green cruciferous vegetable loaded with vitamins (especially vitamins K, A and C), iron, and antioxidants. It helps with liver detoxification and also has anti-inflammatory properties. Add 1-3 tablespoons of minced or chopped kale to your pet's food daily, depending on body

weight, as a great source of fiber, nutrients and whole food antioxidants.

7. **Kefir** is a fermented milk beverage that contains beneficial probiotics that support the immune system. Although regular, pasteurized cow's milk can be irritating to pets' GI tracts, and is not recommended for cats, fermented milk is different. One of the best and least expensive ways to get healthy bacteria through your pet's diet is to convert raw milk to kefir yourself. All you need is one-half packet of kefir starter granules in a quart of raw milk (preferably organic and if possible, raw cat milk), which you leave at room temperature overnight. Add 1-3 teaspoons of this super probiotic to your pet's food 1-2 times daily for overall improved GI defenses (most of your pet's immunologic health is located in her GI tract, so a healthy gut = a healthy pet!).

8. **Pepitas** or raw pumpkin seeds, are a rich source of minerals, vitamin K, and phytosterols. They also contain L-tryptophan and are a good source of zinc, vitamin E, and B vitamins. Research suggests pumpkin seeds can prevent calcium oxalate kidney stones, reduce

inflammation caused by arthritis, and support prostate health.

9. **Sardines.** Fish are a rich source of omega-3 fatty acids, which are essential to your pet's well-being. If you supplement your pet's diet with fish, I suggest you use sardines packed in water. Sardines don't live long enough to store toxins in their bodies, and they're a terrific source of omega-3s.

10. **Sweet potatoes** are rich in beta-carotene and antioxidants, and are also high in vitamins A and C. Sweet potatoes with purple flesh have potent antioxidant and anti-inflammatory properties that may lower the risk from heavy metals and oxygen radicals.

Potentially Dangerous Foods

It is just a Treat – Right?

Be sure that you follow some basic guidelines about wellness. First, don't make food treats a substitute for physical activity.

"To me, a pet treat is a special event that may or may not have to do with food," says Tony Buffington, DVM, professor of veterinary clinical sciences at Ohio State University. "There are so many fat pets out there; simply interacting with your pet is a wonderful thing."

Because treats should make up only a very small fraction of total calories that your pet consumes, it isn't important that they be nutritionally complete. Treats are not meal repalcements. Your primary concern should be portion control, staying mindful about ingredient safety and the high quality of ingredients you are using to make your homemade treats. Obesity amoung humans and pets is an epidemic in the United States and no one wants to cause their family member to become obese or to become a diabetic. Yes even our pets are now becoming diabetic.

Know Your Potentially Harmful Ingredients

There is a brief section in this book about things we know cats should not eat. However, and more importantly, the American Society for the Prevention of Cruelty to Animals maintains a list of problematic foods that you may want to avoid using in your recipes, especially if you know your pet has food sensitivities.

The web site is: http://www.aspca.org/pet-care/animal-poison-control/people-foods-avoid-feeding-your-pets

Milk, for example, is often used as a binder in biscuit recipes, but in small amounts that shouldn't cause digestive issues. However, in each recipe where dairy was called for, we substituted Goat Milk or Cheese.

"The dose makes the poison," Tony says. "There are published toxicity levels for most of the ASPCA-listed ingredients, and often they're higher than what your pet is likely to eat in a small snack offered as an occasional treat."

Still, if you're worried about any ingredient, leave it out. Or come up with a substitute that will work for you and your pet like we did with dairy milk and goat milk and cheese.

Potentially Dangerous Foods for your Cat

Because they're such picky eaters, we sometimes think cats know what's best for them when it's time to eat.

But the fact that they'll walk away from a piece of bad meat doesn't mean they'll bypass an open can of tuna.

Even the can of tuna can be just as dangerous. In fact, you may be surprised to learn some of the common foods your cats should never eat.

Tuna: There are recipes for tuna treats in this book. They are intended to be treats not meal replacements.

Cats can be addicted to tuna, whether it's packed for cats or for humans. Some small tuna treats now and then are okay. But a steady diet of tuna prepared for humans can lead to malnutrition because it won't have all the nutrients a cat needs and too much tuna can cause mercury poisoning.

Onions, Garlic, Chives: Onion in all forms -- powdered, raw, cooked, or dehydrated -- can break down a cat's red blood cells, leading to anemia. That's true even for the onion powder that's found in some baby foods. An occasional small dose probably won't hurt. But eating a large quantity once or eating smaller amounts regularly can cause onion poisoning. Along with onions, garlic and chives can cause gastrointestinal upset.

Milk and Other Dairy Products: What could be wrong with offering your cat a saucer of milk or a piece of cheese? Most cats are lactose-intolerant. Their digestive system cannot process dairy foods, and the result can be digestive upset with diarrhea.

Alcohol: Beer, liquor, wine, foods containing alcohol -- none of it is good for your cat. That's because alcohol has the same effect on a cat's liver and brain that it has on humans. But it takes far less to do its damage. Just two teaspoons of whisky can cause a coma in a 5-pound cat, and one more teaspoon could kill it. The higher the proof, the worse the symptoms.

Grapes and Raisins: Grapes and raisins have often been used as treats for pets. But it's not a good idea. Although it isn't clear why, grapes and raisins can cause kidney failure in cats. And, a small amount can make a cat ill. Repeated vomiting and hyperactivity are early signs. Although some cats show no ill effects, it's best not to give your cat any grapes and to keep grapes and raisins off countertops and other places accessible to your cat.

Caffeine: Caffeine in large enough quantities can be fatal for a cat and there is no antidote. Symptoms of caffeine poisoning include restlessness, rapid breathing, heart palpitations, muscle tremors and fits. In addition to tea and coffee -- including beans and grounds -- caffeine can be found in cocoa, chocolate, colas, and stimulant drinks such as Red Bull. It's also in some cold medicines and painkillers.

Chocolate: Chocolate can be lethal for cats. Although most cats won't eat it on their own, they can be coaxed to eat it by owners and others who think they are giving the cat a treat. The toxic agent in chocolate is theobromine.

It's in all kinds of chocolate, even white chocolate. The most dangerous kinds, are dark chocolate and unsweetened baking chocolate. Eating chocolate can cause abnormal heart rhythm, tremors, seizures, and death.

Candy and Gum: Candy, gum, toothpaste, baked goods, and some diet foods are sweetened with xylitol. Xylitol can cause an increase in the insulin circulating through your cat's body, which will cause the cat's blood sugar to drop. Xylitol can also lead to liver failure. Initial symptoms include vomiting, lethargy, and loss of coordination. The cat may have seizures soon after ingesting the xylitol, and liver failure can occur within just a few days.

Fat Trimmings and Bones: Table scraps often contain fat trimmed off of meat and bones. Both fat and bones may be dangerous for cats. Fat, both cooked and uncooked, can cause intestinal upset, with vomiting and diarrhea. And a cat can choke on a bone. Bones can also splinter and cause an obstruction or lacerations of your cat's digestive system.

Raw Eggs: There are two problems with giving your cat raw eggs. The first is the possibility of food poisoning from bacteria like salmonella or *E. coli*. The second is a rarer problem. There is a protein in raw egg whites, called avidin which could interfere with the absorption of the B vitamin biotin. This can cause skin problems as well as problems with your cat's coat.

Raw Meat and Fish: There is a great deal of debate over raw food diets lately. You can of course research more into that as an option. Cats in the wild certainly eat raw meat and fish.

However, the current view for domestic inside pets is that raw meat and raw fish, like raw eggs, can contain bacteria that cause food poisoning. In addition, an enzyme in raw fish destroys thiamine, which is an essential B vitamin for your cat.

A lack of thiamine can cause serious neurological problems and lead to convulsions and coma.

Dog Food: An occasional bite of dog food won't hurt your cat. But dog food is not a substitute for cat food. They do have many of the same ingredients.

Cat food is specially formulated for a cat's needs, which include more protein as well as certain vitamins and fatty acids. A steady diet of dog food can cause your cat to be severely malnourished and in some cases coma.

Liver: As with Tuna, small amounts of liver are okay, but eating too much liver can cause vitamin A toxicity. This is a serious condition that can affect your cat's bones. Symptoms include deformed bones, bone growths on the elbows and spine, and osteoporosis. Vitamin A toxicity can also cause death.

Too Many Treats: Eating too much too often can do the same thing to cats that it does to humans. It can lead to obesity and even diabetes.

Yeast Dough: Before it's baked, bread dough needs to rise. And, that's exactly what it would do in your cat's stomach if your cat ate it. As it swells inside, the dough can stretch the abdomen and cause severe pain. In addition, when the yeast ferments the dough to make it rise, it produces alcohol that can lead to alcohol poisoning.

Your Medicine: Ingesting a drug prescribed for humans is one of the most common causes of poisoning in cats. Just as you would do for your children, put all medicines where your cat can't get to them and never give your cat any over-the-counter medicine unless advised to do so by your vet. Ingredients such as acetaminophen or ibuprofen are common in pain relievers and cold medicine. They can be deadly for your cat.

Kitchen Pantry: No Cats Allowed: Many other items commonly found on kitchen shelves can harm your cat. Keeping food items where your cat can't get to them and keeping pantry and cupboard doors closed will help protect your cat from serious food-related illness.

If Your Cat Eats What It Shouldn't: No matter how cautious you are, it's possible your cat can find and swallow what it shouldn't. It's a smart idea to always keep the numbers of your local vet, the closest emergency clinic, and the **ASPCA Animal Poison Control Center -- (888) 426-4435** -- where you know you can find them in an emergency. If you think your cat has consumed something that's toxic, call for emergency help at once.

What Cats Can Eat: Cats are carnivores and need meat. Talking with your vet about the cat food you provide and following the directions on the label will help ensure your cat's diet is balanced and your cat stays healthy.

Grain Free

Because Cats are obligate carnivores and have developed various sensitivity issues, as a result of being raised by humans and from consuming poor quality commercial pet products, grain free cat food is becoming more and more popular among pet parents, but is it a good choice? Learn here how to choose the best diet for your cat.

There is a lot of talk in the pet community about grain free foods, and you might be wondering what's causing all the hype. Many scientists believe that a grain free diet is more appropriate for cats because they are carnivores, and foods rich in proteins rather than grain-based carbohydrates more closely resemble their natural diet.

Grains like corn, wheat, and rice are the foundations for many cat foods. This is because they are cheap to produce and allow the food manufacturer to meet the carbohydrate requirements for their foods while saving some money.

These types of grains, however, can cause problems for some cats. Some cats are allergic to grains, and others have a hard time digesting them. Some scientists believe that this is because cats weren't designed to do so -- they lack a salivary enzyme called amylase that helps to break down carbohydrates like corn and wheat before they reach the stomach. Cats do, however, use amylase secreted by the pancreas during digestion in the intestines.

A wild cat's natural diet would contain more protein, and they would likely ingest only small amounts of carbohydrates through the proteins (or animals) they consumed.

Grain free diets can contain more of the ingredients that your cat would be eating in the wild. Proteins like fish and meat are found in greater amounts in some grain free foods. However, some manufacturers of grain free foods simply substitute other highly glycemic carbohydrate sources like potato and tapioca, which are similar to grains in their nutrient makeup.)

Some cats develop an allergy to grains, and grain free diets aim to eliminate the ingredients causing the sensitivity.

Because grain free foods can be higher in protein, they can also be higher in fat. Be sure that you are feeding your cat the appropriate portion size so that they do not put on weight.

Grain free foods that contain more protein will likely be more expensive. However, you will probably be feeding your cat smaller portions because of the high protein, so this may make up for the price difference.

Talk to your veterinarian about whether a grain free food is a good choice for your cat, and ask for brand recommendations. When shopping for grain free cat food, be careful not to be tricked by labels that say "all natural" or promise to make your cat healthier than anything else out there. You can get the full story by checking out the ingredients and nutrient analysis on the back of the bag or can.

Just because a food is grain free doesn't mean it will be right for your cat. Always check with your veterinarian before switching your cat to a new type of diet.

Pottenger's Cats: A study in Nutrition

Recomended Reading

Pottenger's Cats: A Study in Nutrition
2nd Edition

by Francis Marion Pottenger Jr.

ISBN-13: 978-0916764067

ISBN-10: 0916764060

A comparison of healthy cats on raw foods and those on heated diets. Behavioral characteristics, arthritis, sterility, skeletal deformities and allergies are some of the problems that are associated with the consumption of cooked foods.

Book Review by Pat McKay

Francis Pottenger, Jr, MD, has given the cat world one of the best books available in the study of carnivore's nutrition. Between the years of 1932 and 1942, he conducted a feeding experiment to determine the effects of heat-processed food on 900 cats. I have to admit I don't like the reason he was doing the study, because it involved adrenalectomies (surgical removal of the adrenal glands) for use in standardizing the hormone content of the adrenal extract he was making. However, the study tells so much about carnivorous cats and their need for raw food that as long as the study has already been done, let's now make this information useful for cats.

Most of what I have written in this article/review is verbatim from his book. The complete 123 page book is available from the Price-Pottenger Nutrition Foundation for $9.95.

http://www.ppnf.org/catalog/ppnf/index.htm

The cats in the study were kept in large outdoor pens overlooking the San Gabriel Valley in California, so the weather was moderate for the cats. Each pen had an open air enclosure 12 feet long, 6 feet wide, and 7 feet high which was screened by chicken-wire so the cats had adequate exposure to the sun. A trench 18 inches deep was dug in each enclosure and filled with freshly washed sand. A roofed area approximately 4 feet deep with a wooden floor and bedding extended from the back of each pen to provide shelter for the animals during inclement weather.

All animals were subject to the same routine procedures. Each cat had its own clinical chart and notes were kept through his/her life. At the end of ten years, 600 out of 900 cats studied had complete, recorded health histories.

GENERAL OBSERVATIONS

RAW MEAT GROUP

The cats fed a diet of 2/3 raw meat, 1/3 raw milk, and cod liver oil show striking uniformity in their sizes and their skeletal developments. From generation to generation they maintain a regular, broad face with prominent malar (pertaining to the cheek or cheek bone) and orbital arches, adequate nasal cavities, broad dental arches, and regular dentition. The configuration of the female skull is different from the male skull, and each sex maintains his/her distinct anatomical features. The membranes are firm and of good, pink color with no evidence of infection or degenerative change. Tissue tone is excellent, and the fur is of good quality with very little shedding noted. In the older cats, particularly the males, engaging in fighting, the incisors are often missing, but inflammation and disease of the gums is seldom seen.

The calcium and phosphorus content of their femurs remains consistent, and their internal organs show full development and normal function. Over their life spans, they prove resistant to infections, to fleas, and to various other parasites, and show no signs of allergies. In general, they are gregarious, friendly, and predictable in their behavior patterns, and when thrown or dropped as much as six feet to test their coordination, they always land on their feet and come back for more play. These cats reproduce one homogeneous generation after another with the average weight of the kittens at birth being 119 grams. Miscarriages are rare, and the litters average five kittens with the mother cat nursing her young without difficulty.

COOKED MEAT GROUP

The cats fed a diet of 2/3 cooked meat, 1/3 raw milk, and cod liver oil reproduce a heterogeneous strain of kittens, each kitten in a litter being different in size and skeletal pattern. When comparing the changes in configuration found in their x-rays, there are almost as many variations in the facial and dental structures of the second and third generation cooked-meat fed animals as there are animals. Evidence of deficiencies is written so plainly on their faces that with a little training, any observer can be almost certain that a given cat has been subjected to a deficient diet or that it comes from a line of cats that has suffered from deficient nutrition.

The long bones of cooked-meat cats tend to increase in length and decrease in diameter with the hind legs commonly increasing in length over the forelegs. The trabeculation (the internal structural mesh of the bones) becomes coarser and shows evidence of less calcium. In the third generation, some of the bones become as soft as rubber, and a true condition of osteogenesis imperfecta (the inherited condition in which bones are abnormally brittle and subject to fractures) is present.

Heart problems; nearsightedness and farsightedness; under activity of the thyroid or inflammation of the thyroid gland; infections of the kidney, of the liver, of the testes, of the ovaries, and of the bladder; arthritis and inflammation of the joints; inflammation of the nervous system with paralysis and meningitis—all occur commonly in these cooked-meat-fed cats. A decrease in visceral volume is evidenced by the diminishing size of their thoracic and abdominal cavities.

Frank infections of the bone appear regularly and often appear to be the case of death. By the time the third deficient generation is born, the cats are so physiologically bankrupt that none survive beyond the sixth month of life, thereby terminating the strain.

A study of the microscopic sections of the lungs of second and third generation deficient cats show abnormal respiratory tissues. The lungs show hyperemia, some edema and partial atelectasis (incomplete expansion of lungs at birth), while the most deficient show bronchitis and pneumonitis (localized acute inflammation of the lungs without toxemia). In several cases, a hypothyroid condition exists with the thyroid gland showing scanty colloid and small acini (plural of acinus—one of the small sacs in a gland lining with secreting cells), again not observable in raw-meat-fed cats.

Cooked-meat-fed cats show much more irritability. Some females are even dangerous to handle and three are named Tiger, Cobra, and Rattlesnake because of their proclivity for biting and scratching. The males, on the other hand, are more docile, often to the point of being unaggressive, and their sex interest is slack or perverted. In essence, there is evidence of a role reversal with the female cats becoming the aggressors and the male cats becoming passive as well as evidence of increasing abnormal activities between the same sexes. Such sexual deviations are not observed among the raw- food cats.

Vermin and intestinal parasites abound. Skin lesions and allergies appear frequently and are progressively worse from one generation to the next. Pneumonia and empyema (accumulation of pus in a cavity of the body, especially the chest) are among the principal causes of death in adult cats while diarrhea followed by pneumonia takes a heavy toll on the kittens.

At autopsy, cooked-meat-fed females frequently present ovarian atrophy and uterine congestion, and the males often show failure in the development of active spermatogenesis (process of formation of spermatazoa). (Spermatazoa (plural of Spermatazoon--male germ cells.) Abortion in pregnant females is common, running about 25 percent in the first deficient generation to about 70 percent in the second generation. Deliveries are generally difficult with many females dying in labor. The mortality rate of the kittens also is high as the kittens are either born dead or are born too frail to nurse. Following delivery, a few mother cats steadily decline in health only to die from some obscure physiological exhaustion in about three months. Other cats show increasing difficulty with their pregnancies, and in many instances, fail to become pregnant. The average weight of the kittens born of cooked-meat-fed mothers is 100 grams, 19 grams less than the raw meat nurtured kittens.

REGENERATING CATS

When cats of the first and second generation cooked-meat-fed groups are returned to a raw meat diet, they are classified as regenerating animals of the first and second orders. Their progeny are then maintained on an optimum diet to measure the time needed to rebuild their health to that of the normal cats. It requires approximately four generations for either order to regenerate to a state of normal health. However, because of the lack of reproductive efficiency, very few deficient animals regain the normal health noted before deficiency was imposed on their line of cats.

Improvement in resistance to disease is noted in the second generation regenerating cat, but allergic manifestations persist into the third generation. In the third generation, skeletal and soft tissue changes are still noticeable, but to a lesser degree; and by the fourth, most of the severe deficiency signs and symptoms disappear—but seldom completely.

One of the experiment's more startling discoveries is that once a female cat is subjected to a deficient diet for a period of 12 to 18 months, her reproductive efficiency is so reduced that she is never again able to give birth to normal kittens. Even after three or four years of eating an optimum diet, her kittens still show signs of deficiency in skeletal and dental development. When her kittens are maintained on an optimum diet, a gradual reversal and regeneration takes place.

The only other portion of this book I want to bring forth just to show the difference in all the types of processed milk and that what we call "milk" now is really no longer a food and can cause serious problems for cats, dogs, and/or people.

THE RAW MILK VERSUS COOKED MILK FEEDING EXPERIMENT

This feeding experiment involves four groups of cats. One group received a diet of 2/3 raw milk, 1/3 raw meat, and cod liver oil. The other groups receive a diet of either 2/3 pasteurized milk, 2/3 evaporated milk, or 2/3 sweetened condensed milk, plus 1/3 raw meat, and cod liver oil.

The results of this experiment correspond to those of the raw meat versus cooked meat experiment. Animals on raw milk and raw meat reproduce homogeneous litters, and the usual causes of death are old age and injuries suffered in fighting. They are generally healthy animals with normal anatomic measurements and good resistance to disease. Their fur is of good quality with a notable sheen, and they show no signs of allergy.

The cats fed pasteurized milk as the principal item of their diet show skeletal changes, lessened reproductive efficiency, and their kittens present progressive constitutional and respiratory problems as is evident in the first, second, and third generation deficient cats eating cooked meat.

Cats fed evaporated milk show even more damage than their pasteurized counterparts while the most marked deficiencies occur among those fed sweetened condensed milk. The cats on sweetened condensed milk develop much heavier fat deposits and exhibit severe skeletal deformities. They show extreme irritability and pace back and forth in their pens.

"With all the excellent information provided in Dr. Pottenger's ten years of study, it is eminently clear that canned, dry, and cooked foods, including pasteurized and other processed milk, are not for cats.", Pat McKay.

Bibliography, Credits & Resources

Bibliography, Credits and Resources

This book is an adaptation, assembly and an accumulation of thoughts, ideas, articals and excerpts, facts, recipes and information from the public domain collected and assembled under the Fair Use for Education and Research Act from various public domain resoures and sites including but not limited to:

"Welcome to AAFCO." *The Association of American Feed Control Officials Home.* N.p., n.d. Web. 30 Mar. 2016.

Becker, Karen. "Nutritious and Delicious Pet Treats You Can Make in a Flash." *Mercola.com.* N.p., 10 Feb. 2012. Web. 30 Mar. 2016.

"GMO Facts." *The NonGMO Project RSS.* N.p., n.d. Web. 30 Mar. 2016.

"National Organic Program." *National Organic Program.* N.p., n.d. Web. 30 Mar. 2016.

Nelsheim, Malden C., PhD, and Marion Nestle. "Natural, Human Grade, Organic Dog

Food: Really?" *The Bark*. N.p., n.d. Web. 30 Mar. 2016.

"10 Human Superfoods Perfect for Sharing with Your Pet." *Mercola.com*. N.p., n.d. Web. 30 Mar. 2016.

Alling, Meredith. "Is Grain Free Cat Food a Good Choice?" *Is Grain Free Cat Food a Good Choice?* N.p., 06 Jan. 2014. Web. 30 Mar. 2016.

Beuerlein, Karen. "How to Make All-Natural Pet Treats." *DIY*. N.p., n.d. Web. 30 Mar. 2016.

"U.S. Department of Agriculture." *U.S. Department of Agriculture*. N.p., n.d. Web. 30 Mar. 2016.

"GMO Awareness." *GMO Awareness*. N.p., n.d. Web. 30 Mar. 2016.

Nestle, Marion. *Pet Food Politics: The Chihuahua in the Coal Mine*. Berkeley: U of California, 2008. Print.

"GMO Facts." *The NonGMO Project RSS*. N.p., n.d. Web. 30 Mar. 2016.

"Pet Health Center." *WebMD*. N.p., n.d. Web. 30 Mar. 2016.

Pottenger, Francis M., Elaine Pottenger, and Robert T. Pottenger. *Pottenger's Cats: A Study in Nutrition*. La Mesa, CA (P.O. Box 2614, La Mesa 92041): Price-Pottenger Nutrition Foundation, 1983. Print.

Mckay, Book Review By Pat. "Pottenger's Cats Book Review." *Pottenger's Cats A Study in Nutrition* (n.d.): n. pag. *Http://www.ectownusa.net*. Web.

www.ingramcontent.com/pod-product-compliance
Lightning Source LLC
Chambersburg PA
CBHW052059110526
44591CB00013B/2272